THE YELLOW·JAR

Also available:
The Fairy Tales of Oscar Wilde
by P. Craig Russell, vols. 1, 2, 3: $15.95 each
Sundiata, an African Tale by Will Eisner: $15.95

($3 P&H 1st item, $1 each addt'l)

We have over 150 graphic
novels in print, write
for our color catalog:
NBM, dept. S
555 8th Ave., Suite 1202
New York, NY 10018
www.nbmpublishing.com
www.atangan.com

ISBN 1-56163-331-3
© 2002 Patrick Atangan
Printed in Hong Kong

5   4   3   2

Library of Congress Cataloging-in-Publication Data

Atangan, Patrick.
    The yellow jar / Patrick Atangan.
        p.cm.
        ISBN 1-56163-331-3 (hc.)
        I. Title.

PN6727.A87 Y45 2003
741.5'973--dc21

2002032132

THE YELLOW·JAR

TWO·TALES·FROM·JAPANESE·TRADITION

VOLUME I

PATRICK·ATANGAN

NANTIER · BEALL · MINOUSTCHINE
Publishing inc.
new york

Introduction by P. Craig RUSSELL

A few years ago, fellow cartoonist Brian Apthorp sent me a package containing drawing samples of a young student of his. Seeing similarities of temperament, style, and influence between Patrick's work and my own, particularly that of Japanese woodblock prints and European Art Nouveau (what he sent me was a Batman story drawn in the style of an Art Nouveau stained glass window), he asked if I might have any suggestions for the obviously talented young artist. Patrick and I eventually made contact and he began sending me copies of his latest work through the mail and by e-mail.

Unlike so many young artists over the years who have shown me their work with a request for a critique and who I've spent an hour or two with, making suggestions on storytelling techniques, composition, layout, etc., and who go off and are never heard from again, Patrick actually addressed the new challenges and possibilities presented to him and returned in a few weeks or a month or two with an entirely new story. Every new piece presented a significant advance over his previous work. His artistic growth could be charted, literally, on a weekly basis. It was very exciting to witness.

Patrick, being still a somewhat shy young man (this will pass), was hesitant to put himself forward and so it was my pleasure, a couple of years ago, to escort him around the San Diego comic convention and introduce him and his work to the editors of a half dozen or so 'alternative' (i.e. outside the mainstream world of Marvel/DC superhero comics) publishing houses. Several expressed immediate interest in his work and I watched with particular interest as Thierry Nantier of NBM sat down and very carefully addressed his work, criticizing and suggesting, as I happily noticed, with the air of an editor handling the work of an artist who is not being sent back to the studio to try again but is instead being readied for publication.

I think The Yellow Jar, the book that resulted from Patrick and Thierry's initial meeting, is a stellar piece of work and I take great pleasure in being here to toast a young artist's inaugural publication.

Here's to many more.

ONCE UPON A TIME,--

--IN THE LAND NOW KNOWN AS JAPAN,--

--THERE WAS A SMALL AND SLEEPY VILLAGE, KNOWN PRIMARILY FOR ITS EXPORTS OF FINE INDIGO AND CANARY SILKS.

IT IS HERE LIVED A SIMPLE FISHER-MAN,--

--NAMED NIKOTUCHI.

THE ·YELLOW·JAR

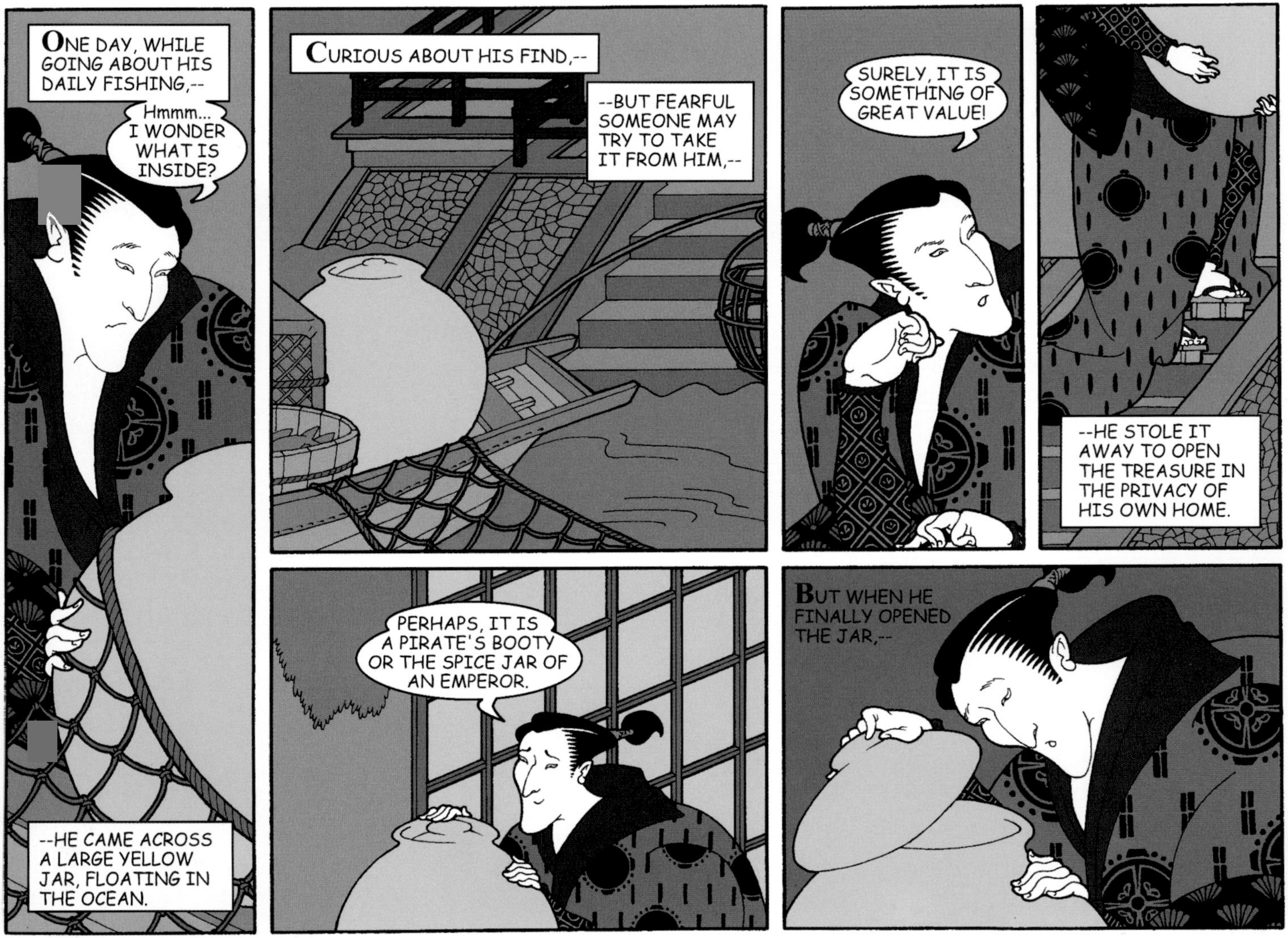
ONE DAY, WHILE GOING ABOUT HIS DAILY FISHING,--
Hmmm... I WONDER WHAT IS INSIDE?
--HE CAME ACROSS A LARGE YELLOW JAR, FLOATING IN THE OCEAN.
CURIOUS ABOUT HIS FIND,--
--BUT FEARFUL SOMEONE MAY TRY TO TAKE IT FROM HIM,--
SURELY, IT IS SOMETHING OF GREAT VALUE!
--HE STOLE IT AWAY TO OPEN THE TREASURE IN THE PRIVACY OF HIS OWN HOME.
PERHAPS, IT IS A PIRATE'S BOOTY OR THE SPICE JAR OF AN EMPEROR.
BUT WHEN HE FINALLY OPENED THE JAR,--

--INSTEAD OF FINDING A STASH OF PEARLS AND GEMS OR AN ASSORTMENT OF RARE HERBS AND SPICES,--

--ALTHOUGH HE DIDN'T REALIZE IT AT THE TIME, NIKOTUCHI FOUND SOMETHING OF EVEN GREATER IMPORTANCE.

WHAT IS THIS? THIS IS NO GREAT TREASURE!

INSIDE THE YELLOW JAR SLEPT A BEAUTIFUL MAIDEN IN A SILKEN YELLOW DRESS.

DISAPPOINTED THAT IT WASN'T TREASURE, HE DECIDED TO KEEP THE JAR AS A REWARD.

HE THEN LEFT THE MAIDEN IN HIS HOUSE AND NERVOUSLY TOOK THE JAR--

Hmmph! NOTHING INDEED!

--AND BURIED IT IN HIS GARDEN UNDER A WILLOW TREE.

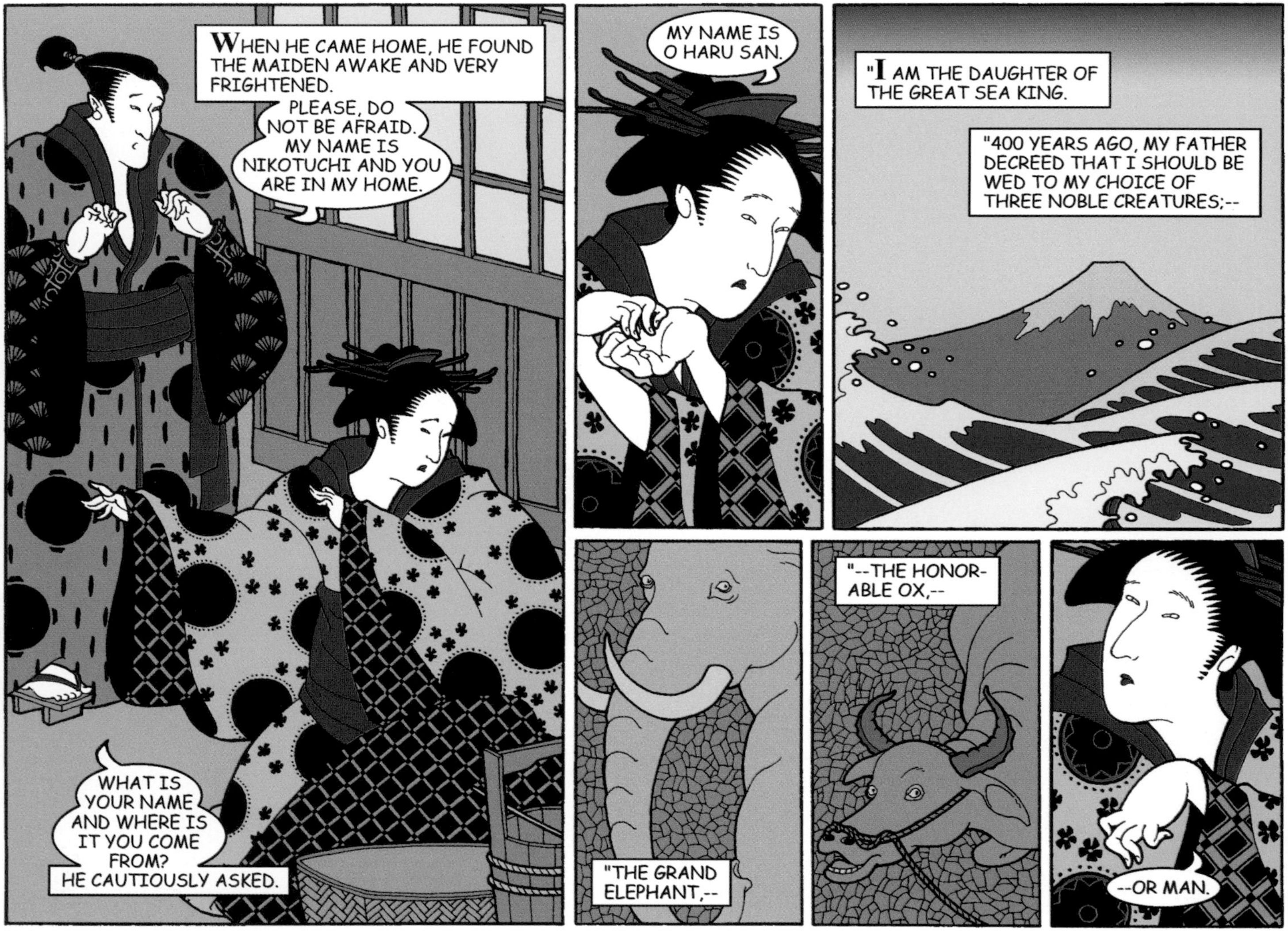
WHEN HE CAME HOME, HE FOUND THE MAIDEN AWAKE AND VERY FRIGHTENED.
PLEASE, DO NOT BE AFRAID. MY NAME IS NIKOTUCHI AND YOU ARE IN MY HOME.
WHAT IS YOUR NAME AND WHERE IS IT YOU COME FROM?
HE CAUTIOUSLY ASKED.
MY NAME IS O HARU SAN.
"I AM THE DAUGHTER OF THE GREAT SEA KING.
"400 YEARS AGO, MY FATHER DECREED THAT I SHOULD BE WED TO MY CHOICE OF THREE NOBLE CREATURES;--
"THE GRAND ELEPHANT,--
"--THE HONOR-ABLE OX,--
--OR MAN.

"MY FATHER THEN GAVE ME A MAGIC JAR SO THAT I MAY TRAVEL ACROSS THE OCEANS IN SEARCH FOR MY MATE.

"I FOUND THE ELEPHANT AND OX AND APPEARED TO THEM AS A COLORFUL HEN. BUT THE GRAND ELEPHANT OFTEN SPOKE TOO GRANDLY OF HIMSELF.

THOU PLUMES MAY BE BRIGHT, O HARU SAN, BUT NONE IS AS BEAUTIFUL AS I.

"--AND THE OX HARDLY SPOKE TO ME AT ALL.

THERE IS NO NEED FOR CHATTER WITH WORK TO BE DONE.

SO, WITH NEITHER AS A SUITABLE MATE, I AM CAST TO ROAM THE SEAS IN SEARCH--

--OF AN IDEAL GROOM.

OH PLEASE, RELEASE ME SO THAT I MAY RETURN TO MY YELLOW JAR AND FIND A HUSBAND!

Not wanting O Haru San to take the jar and leave him with nothing, he told her--

You were separated from your jar at sea.

I had found you floating in the waters near my fishing boat.

--A lie, of course.

Then my quest to find a mate has failed.

For, if I could not find a good husband in the world of beasts, then, I am certain to find nothing but fools in the world of man.

Please, Oharu san, allow me to prove man's worthiness to wed one as glorious as thee.

Wed into the world of man?

I had not seriously considered a man as a groom.

I will marry you on one condition, that you shall always speak the truth to me.

10

So NIKOTUCHI AND THE SEA PRINCESS WERE MARRIED--

--AND THEY LIVED HAPPILY IN HIS HUMBLE HOUSE BY THE SHORE.

--SHE WAS HAPPY, NONETHELESS.

FOR A WHILE, THEIR MARRIAGE WAS PEACEFUL. ALTHOUGH LIFE WAS DIFFICULT AND O HARU SAN WAS UNUSED TO THE HARD WORK AS A FISHERMAN'S WIFE,--

BUT THERE WAS ONE THING THAT BOTHERED HER.

11

WHENEVER O HARU SAN TRIED TO GO INTO NIKOTUCHI'S GARDEN, WHETHER IT WAS FRUIT OR VEGETABLES, HE WOULD TRY TO STOP HER.

OH, PLEASE, O HARU SAN, ALLOW ME.

FOR MONTHS, HER HUSBAND'S ODD BEHAVIOR CONTINUED UNTIL SHE EVENTUALLY BECAME SUSPICIOUS OF HIS INTENTIONS.

WHAT COULD HE BE HIDING?

SO ONE DAY,--

--WHILE NIKOTUCHI HAD GONE FOR HIS MORNING FISHING,--

--SHE SNUCK INTO THE GARDEN TO UNCOVER HIS SECRET.

THE EARTH HERE IS STILL FRESH.

SHE BEGAN TO DIG.

SHE DUG UNTIL HER KNUCKLES TURNED RAW AND BLOODY.

GASP!

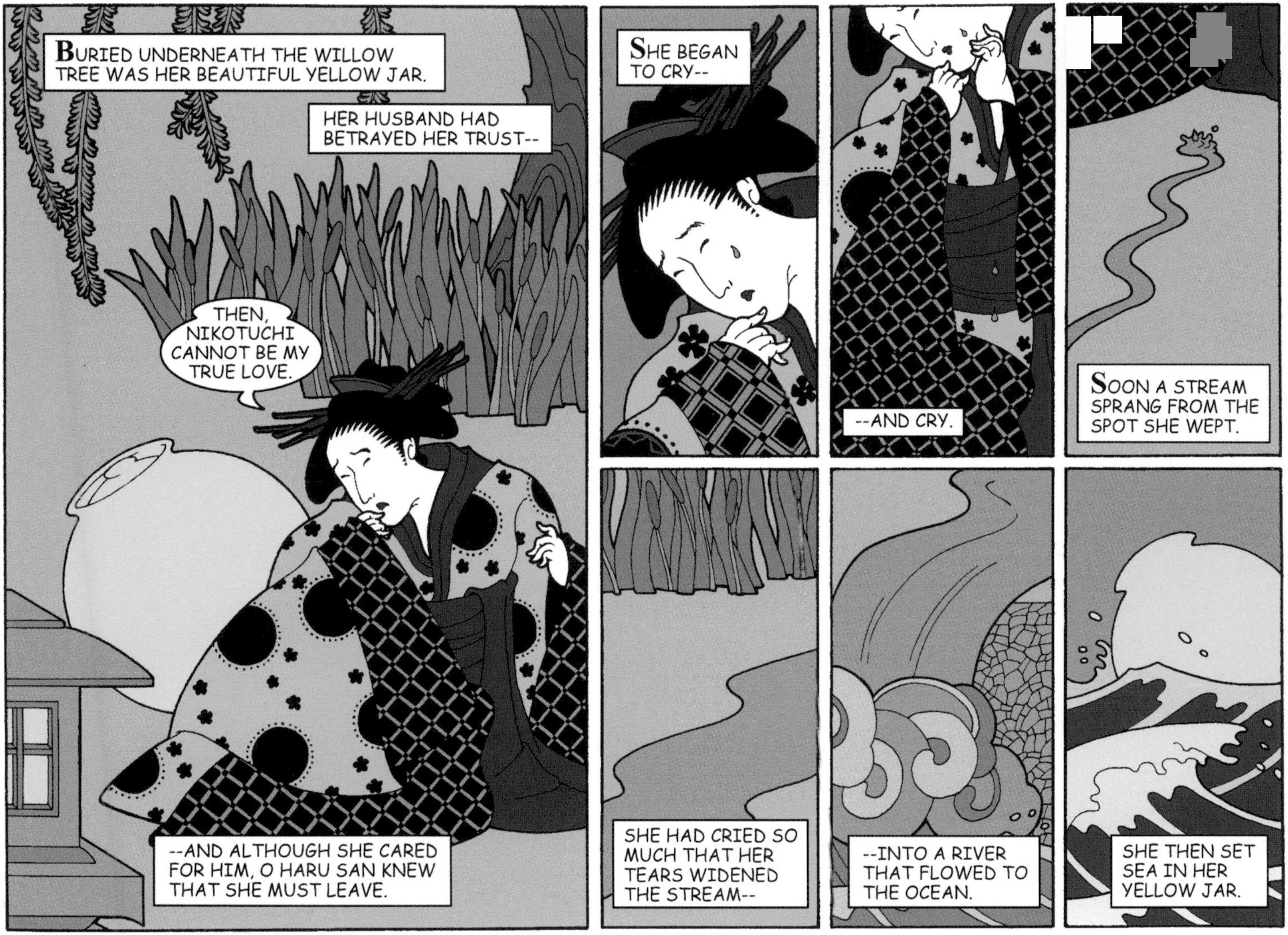

BURIED UNDERNEATH THE WILLOW TREE WAS HER BEAUTIFUL YELLOW JAR.
HER HUSBAND HAD BETRAYED HER TRUST--
THEN, NIKOTUCHI CANNOT BE MY TRUE LOVE.
--AND ALTHOUGH SHE CARED FOR HIM, O HARU SAN KNEW THAT SHE MUST LEAVE.
SHE BEGAN TO CRY--
--AND CRY.
SOON A STREAM SPRANG FROM THE SPOT SHE WEPT.
SHE HAD CRIED SO MUCH THAT HER TEARS WIDENED THE STREAM--
--INTO A RIVER THAT FLOWED TO THE OCEAN.
SHE THEN SET SEA IN HER YELLOW JAR.

W HEN NIKOTUCHI CAME BACK FROM HIS MORNING FISH-
ING, HE NOTICED SOMETHING AMISS. THE HOUSE DID NOT
SMELL OF THE SWEET, PERFUMED STICKY RICE THAT O HARU
SAN USUALLY PREPARED FOR HIM--

--NOR WAS SHE
THERE TO GREET
HIM WITH A KISS.

O HARU SAN HAD LEFT HIM,
BUT EVEN BEFORE NIKOTUCHI
STEPPED INTO HIS GARDEN, HE
ALREADY SUSPECTED WHY.

O HARU SAN?

O HARU SAN?

WITH O HARU SAN GONE, THE HOUSE SEEMED QUIET AND EMPTY.

THE RIVER OF TEARS THAT ONCE FLOWED FROM NIKOTUCHI'S GARDEN--

--HAD DRIED UP INTO A PUDDLE.

--AND FIND O HARU SAN.

FOR DAYS, NIKOTUCHI WASTED AWAY PINING FOR HIS ESTRANGED WIFE,--

--UNTIL, WRECKED BY LONELINESS AND GRIEF, HE FINALLY DECIDED TO SET SEA--

WITH GREAT RESOLVE, NIKOTUCHI BRAVED THE ICY CURRENTS OF THE OCEAN.

HE TRAVELED UNTIL ONE DAY HE FOUND HIMSELF LOST IN A SMALL PORT CITY.

HE SEARCHED FOR THE NEXT THREE YEARS, DESPERATE TO FIND HIS MISSING O HARU SAN. HE TRAVELLED TO STRANGE AND DISTANT LANDS, SAW THE RAREST OF CREATURES AND MET WORLDY PEOPLE OF GREAT RENOWN.

I'M AFRAID I SHALL NEVER FIND MY DEAR O HARU SAN.

WAYWORN AND HUNGRY, NIKOTUCHI WAS ALL ABOUT READY TO GIVE UP, WHEN HE SPIED THE YELLOW JAR IN THE STOREFRONT OF A CURIO SHOP.

O HARU SAN'S JAR!

DO YOU LIKE MY JAR, GOOD TRAVELER? IT IS MADE OF THE FINEST OF STONE.

I ASSURE YOU, IT IS INDEED A RARE FIND, A BEAUTIFULLY CRAFTED REPLICA OF ONE OWNED BY THE GREAT DEMON WARRIOR HOSO NO KAMI.

"BUT HOW MAY I GO ABOUT FINDING THE **ORIGINAL** JAR?" NIKOTUCHI ASKED.

A MAN OF DANGEROUS TASTE, I SEE.

HOSO NO KAMI LIVES ATOP A MOUNTAIN FORTRESS ABOVE THIS VERY TOWN.

ONE MUST TAKE GREAT CARE, FOR HE GUARDS HIS TREASURES JEALOUSLY.

WITH SOME OMINOUS FINAL WORDS, THE SHIFTY-EYED MERCHANT WARNED HIM.

BEWARE TRAVELER, HOSO NO KAMI IS A DEMON! A DEMON, I TELL YOU!

DISTRESSED AT THE POSSIBLE NEWS OF HIS BELOVED O HARU SAN'S FATE, NIKOTUCHI LEFT THE MERCHANT TO MIND HIS STORE.

HE WANDERED THE CITY IN A STUPOR UNTIL--

GASP!

--HE CAME UPON A GANG OF MOURNFUL YOUNG MEN HUD-DLED AT END OF A BLIND ALLEY.

STRICKEN BY THE DEEP SHAME THAT ONLY UNREQUITED LOVE CAN BRING ABOUT, THE MEN HUNG THEIR HEADS WEEPING,--

--BROKEN.

Paaahh! PAY NO ATTENTION TO THESE FOOLS.

18

THESE SORROWFUL SOULS HAVE BEEN ENCHANTED BY THE MOST POWERFUL OF MAGIC, DOOMED TO FOREVER WASTE AWAY, PINING FOR WHAT THEY CAN NEVER POSSESS.

BUT WHAT COULD HAVE REDUCED THEM TO SUCH A STATE?

A WOMAN!

NIKOTUCHI'S EYES LIT UP AT THE MERE POSSIBILITY IT MAY BE HIS WIFE.

A WOMAN?

YES, SOME SAY SHE'S A GODDESS. FOR DAYS NOW, SHE HAS BEEN IMPRISONED BY THE DEMON WARRIOR HOSO NO KAMI.

IF YOU LISTEN, YOU CAN HEAR HER SING OF AN ESTRANGED HUSBAND, WHOM SHE HOPES WILL ONE DAY COME AND RESCUE HER.

THAT IS MY WIFE O HARU SAN! I'VE BEEN IN SEARCH OF HER FOR YEARS!

THEN, IT IS YOU THAT I HAVE BEEN LOOKING FOR.

"FOR YEARS, I HAVE SEARCHED FOR ONE SUCH AS YOU, A MAN WITH PURPOSE ENOUGH TO KILL THE DEMON WARRIOR HOSO NO KAMI."

COME,--

--I'VE SOME-THING TO GIVE YOU.

WHEN HOSO NO KAMI FIRST ARRIVED, HE PILLAGED THE TOWN AND TOOK OUR CROPS. MY HUSBAND WAS ONCE THIS VILLAGE'S GREATEST WARRIOR.

HE FOUGHT BRAVELY AGAINST THE DEMON BUT EVENTUALLY FELL TO HIS SWIFT SWORD. AT THE MOMENT OF MY BELOVED'S DEATH, I CURSED HOSO NO KAMI TO ONE DAY BE SLAIN--

--BY THIS BLADE.

IT WAS MY HUSBAND'S, BUT NOW I GIVE IT TO YOU. TAKE IT, FREE YOUR WIFE--

--AND AVENGE MY HUSBAND'S DEATH!

SO NIKOTUCHI BEGAN THE LONG CLIMB TO THE DEMON'S FORTRESS,--

GREETINGS, GOOD SIR.

--BUT HALFWAY UP THE MOUNTAIN, HE CAME UPON A WEARY LOOKING OX AND A PALE, TREMBLING ELEPHANT CROSSING HIS PATH.

I AM BASHO AND THIS IS MY COMPANION, BUSON. TELL US, STRANGER, WHY DO YOU TREK THIS PATH?

DO YOU HAVE BUSINESS WITH THE WARRIOR WHO LIVES ATOP THE MOUNTAIN?

MY NAME IS NIKOTUCHI AND YES,--

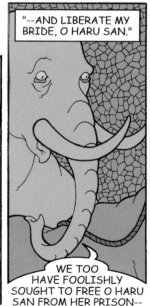

--ALTHOUGH I AM BUT A SIMPLE FISHERMAN AND HE WILL LIKELY SLAY ME, I'VE COME TO CONFRONT THE DEMON-WARRIOR HOSO NO KAMI--

"--AND LIBERATE MY BRIDE, O HARU SAN."

WE TOO HAVE FOOLISHLY SOUGHT TO FREE O HARU SAN FROM HER PRISON--

--FOR WE ARE HER FIRST AND SECOND HUSBANDS.

YET, LIKE YOU, THROUGH OUR OWN FOOLISHNESS,--

--WE LOST O HARU SAN.

"WHEN SHE WAS MY BRIDE, SHE WOULD APPEAR TO ME AS A BEAUTIFUL HEN.

"SHE WOULD SCATTER FLOWER PETALS BEFORE MY FEET DAILY. BUT MY VANITY BLINDED ME TO MY HUSBANDLY DUTIES AND FEELING IGNORED, SHE LEFT ME."

THEN, THE OX SPOKE, "WHEN SHE WAS MY BRIDE,--

"--SHE WOULD FOLLOW MY PLOW WITH SEED. BUT IN MY DESIRE TO SOW THE CROP, I DID NOT SEE HER UNHAPPINESS AND SHE LEFT ME AS WELL."

HOPING SHE WOULD TAKE US BACK, WE TRIED TO FREE HER FROM CAPTIVITY,--

--BUT THE DEMON HOSO NO KAMI IS TOO FIERCE A WARRIOR.

HE HAS TURNED ME PALE IN FEAR.

AND HE HAS BROKEN MY BACK. TELL ME, WHAT GOOD ARE WE NOW TO ANYONE AS A COWARDLY ELEPHANT AND A LAME OX.

BE WARNED NIKOTUCHI, BATTLING HOSO NO KAMI IS A LOST CAUSE.

WITH THOSE WORDS OF WARNING, NIKOTUCHI CONTINUED HIS JOURNEY.

WITH A MIXED SENSE OF FEAR AND ELATION OF AT LAST FINDING HIS WIFE,--

--AND AS THE NIGHT FELL ON THE SKY, AS IF BY SOME DARK FORCE OF MAGIC,--

--NIKOTUCHI CAUTIOUSLY BRAVED THE BRIDGE TO THE DEMON'S FORTRESS--

HOSO NO KAMI!

--HIS FEAR GREW MORE AND MORE.

MY NAME IS NIKOTUCHI AND I'VE COME TO CHALLENGE YOU FOR THE FREEDOM OF MY WIFE, O HARU SAN!

THE DEMON-WARRIOR'S ONLY RESPONSE TO NIKOTUCHI'S CHALLENGE WAS THE SLOW CREAK OF THE DOOR, THAT SEEMED TO GROWL AS IT OPENED.

"NIKOTUCHI!"-- --A VOICE RANG OUT IN A THUNDEROUS BOOM.

THEN THERE WAS NOTHING BUT SILENCE.

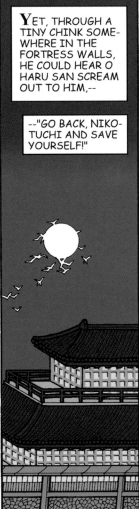

YET, THROUGH A TINY CHINK SOMEWHERE IN THE FORTRESS WALLS, HE COULD HEAR O HARU SAN SCREAM OUT TO HIM,--

--"GO BACK, NIKOTUCHI AND SAVE YOURSELF!"

IN THE SHADOW OF THE GREAT DOORWAY EMERGED--

--THE FORMIDABLE FIGURE OF THE DEMON-WARRIOR HOSO NO KAMI.

SO, FISHERMAN, YOU DARE CHALLENGE ME IN BATTLE?

I BELIEVE, I SHALL ENJOY SLAYING THE FAVORED HUSBAND OF THE BEAUTIFUL O HARU SAN!

ALTHOUGH NIKOTUCHI HAD FOUGHT BRAVELY,--

--HE QUICKLY FELL TO HOSO NO KAMI'S SWIFT SWORD.

YOU ARE A VALIANT FOOL, FISHERMAN, BUT NEITHER BRAVERY NOR DISREGARD FOR YOUR OWN LIFE WILL DEFEAT ME IN BATTLE.

MY SWORD HAS SLAIN MANY LIKE YOU BEFORE.

SHALL YOU GIVE ME REASON TO SPARE **YOU** FROM SUCH A FATE?

POSTURE ALL YOU WANT DEMON, YOU SHALL NOT HEAR ME BEG FOR MY LIFE!

"HAD YOU STARTED TO BEG, I WOULD HAVE MOST CERTAINLY KILLED YOU.

"NOW, COLLECT YOUR REFUSE AND LEAVE ME BE."

O HARU SAN IS **MY** BRIDE NOW!

WITH SHOULDERS SLUMPED AND SHAMED BY DEFEAT, NIKOTUCHI RE-LUCTANTLY LEFT THE FORTRESS AND HIS IMPRISONED WIFE.

THE NEXT EVENING, NIKOTUCHI SNUCK BACK TO THE MOUNTAIN FORTRESS INTENT ON TAKING BACK HIS WIFE.

IF I CANNOT WIN HER FREEDOM, I SHALL STEAL HER AWAY.

HE SEARCHED HALF THE NIGHT FOR A WEAKNESS IN THE PALACE WALL, WITH WHICH HE COULD GAIN ENTRANCE.

WHAT IS THIS?

A CHINK IN THE STONE WALL!

MY PATIENCE WITH YOU WEARS THIN, O HARU SAN. I SHALL ASK YOU AGAIN, AS I HAVE FOR THE LAST FIVE MOONS. WILL YOU ACCEPT ME AS YOUR BRIDE-GROOM?

AND WITH THE FIFTH MOON AS MY WITNESS, I REJECT YOU AS MY HUSBAND.

THEN IT IS HERE IN THIS PRISON YOU SHALL STAY UNTIL YOU AGREE. YOU ARE FOOLISH TO DENY ME SO LONG.

"IT WOULD BE WISE OF YOU TO CHANGE YOUR MIND, LEST MY SWORD BECOMES CARELESS WITH YOUR HUSBANDS NECK!"

HE THEN LEFT O HARU SAN TO CRY HERSELF TO SLEEP.

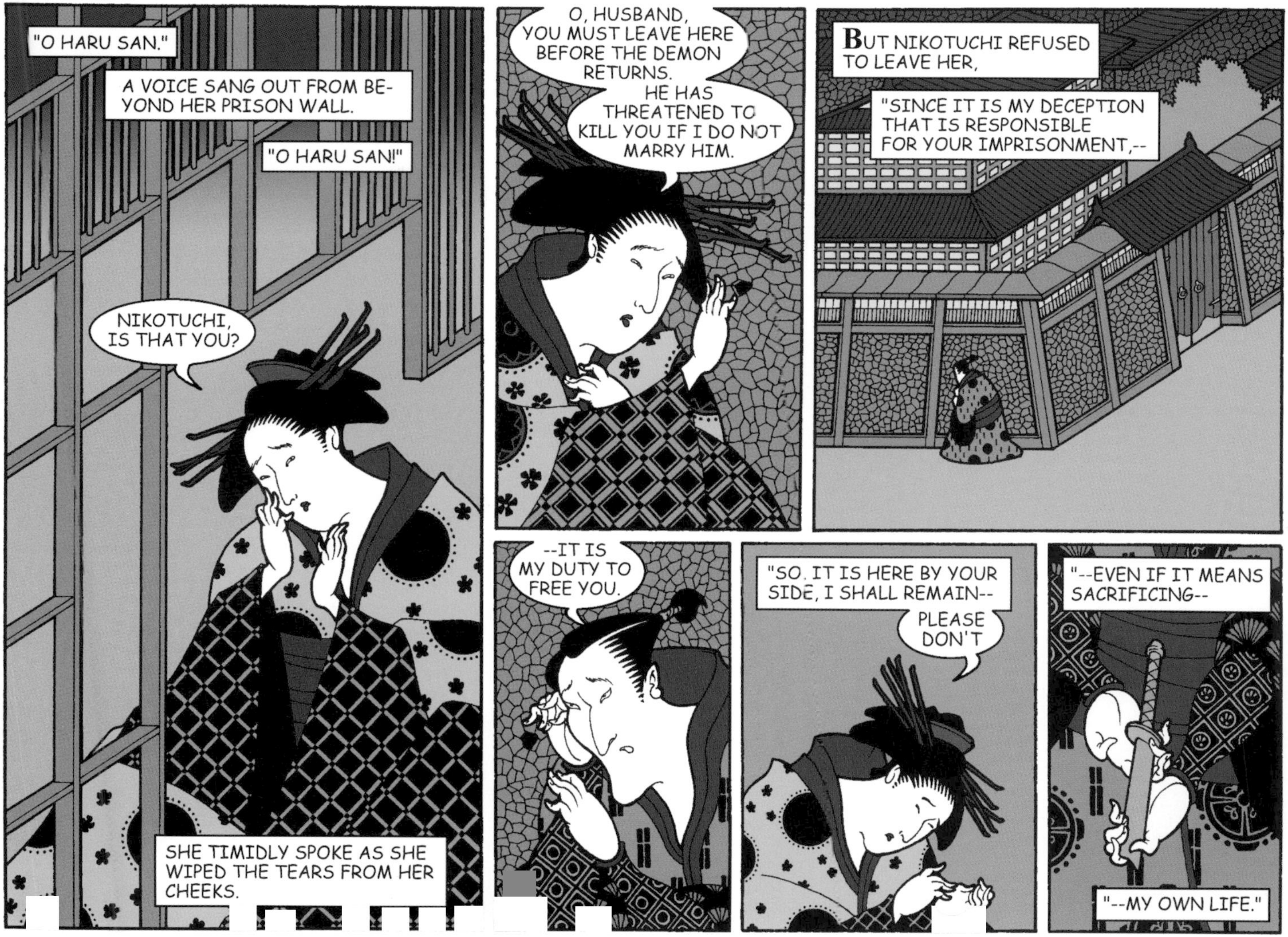
"O HARU SAN."
A VOICE SANG OUT FROM BEYOND HER PRISON WALL.
"O HARU SAN!"
NIKOTUCHI, IS THAT YOU?
SHE TIMIDLY SPOKE AS SHE WIPED THE TEARS FROM HER CHEEKS.
O, HUSBAND, YOU MUST LEAVE HERE BEFORE THE DEMON RETURNS.
HE HAS THREATENED TO KILL YOU IF I DO NOT MARRY HIM.
BUT NIKOTUCHI REFUSED TO LEAVE HER,
"SINCE IT IS MY DECEPTION THAT IS RESPONSIBLE FOR YOUR IMPRISONMENT,--
--IT IS MY DUTY TO FREE YOU.
"SO, IT IS HERE BY YOUR SIDE, I SHALL REMAIN--
PLEASE DON'T
"--EVEN IF IT MEANS SACRIFICING--
"--MY OWN LIFE."

THE FOLLOWING NIGHT,--

--TRUE TO HIS WORD, NIKOTUCHI RETURNED--

--TO DEMON-WARRIOR HOSO NO KAMI'S MOUNTAIN-TOP FORTRESS.

ALTHOUGH HE WAS SURE OF OWN HIS FATE,--

--HE PRESSED FORWARD--

--ARMED WITH LITTLE MORE BUT A BROKEN SWORD, REMINDING HIM OF HIS PROMISE.

HE ARRIVED AT THE GATE ATOP THE GRAND ELEPHANT, BASHO--

--AND, ENSURING HIS O HARU SAN'S FREEDOM, BY HIS SIDE MARCHED BUSON, THE HONORABLE OX--

--AND A HORDE OF ANGRY VILLAGERS WHOM HOSO NO KAMI HAD WRONGED OVER THE YEARS.

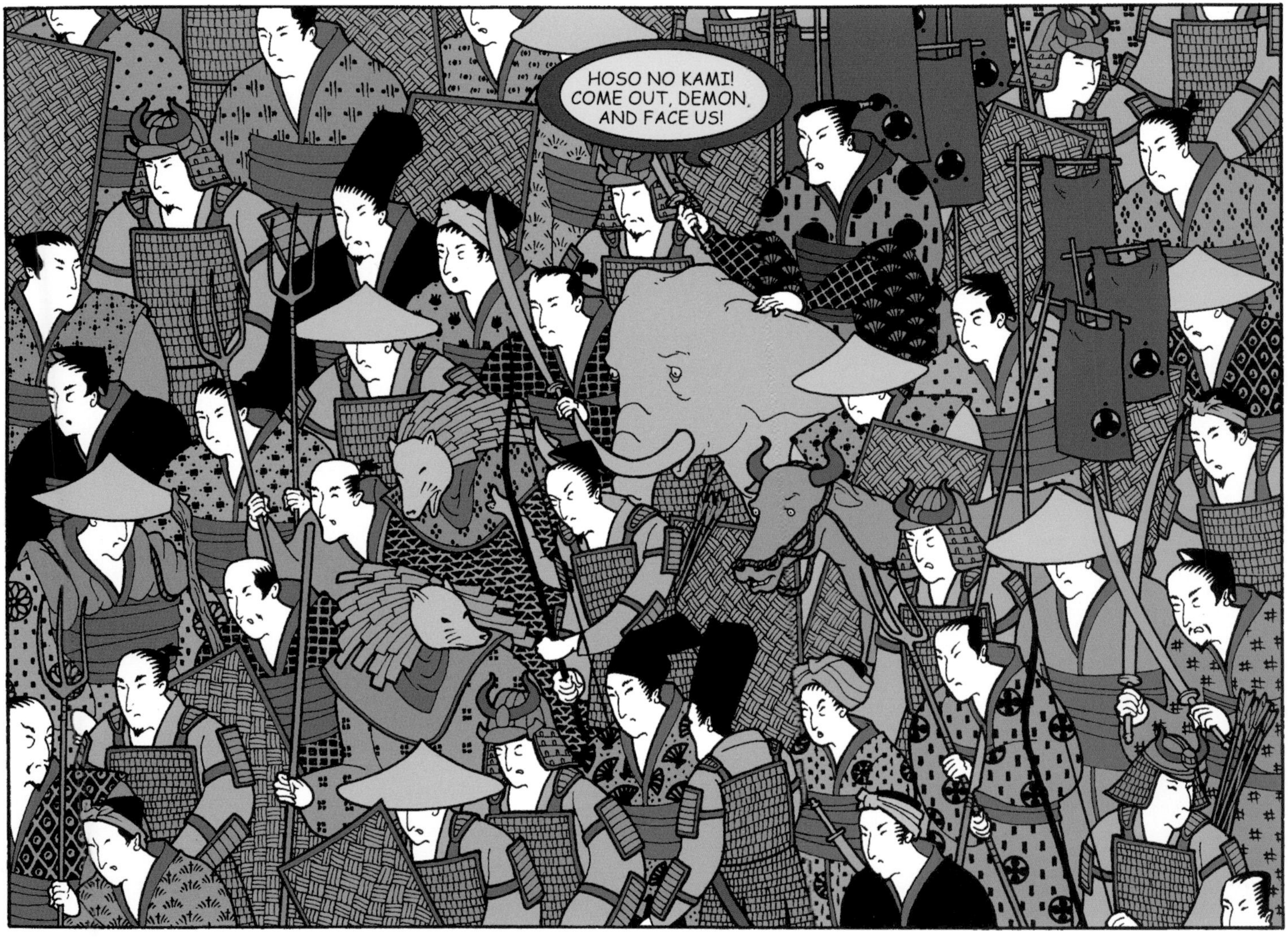
HOSO NO KAMI! COME OUT, DEMON, AND FACE US!

A RUMBLING ERUPTED FROM BEHIND THE FORTRESS GATE.

SLOWLY, THE DOOR YAWNED OPEN.

GREETINGS NIKOTUCHI. I SEE YOU HAVE BROUGHT OTHERS LIKE YOU AS EAGER TO MEET THEIR DEATHS.

IT IS YOU THAT SHALL DIE TONIGHT, HOSO NO KAMI!

DO YOU REALLY THINK YOU AND YOUR PITIFUL BAND OF PEASANTS CAN DEFEAT ME? COME, PUNY HUMANS.

NIKOTUCHI LED A BRAVE FIGHT AGAINST THE DEMON--

--BUT THEY DID LITTLE TO HARM HIM, MUCH LESS FREE O HARU SAN.

FOR HOURS, THE BATTLE WAGED, BUT LITTLE--

--WAS DONE TO QUELL HOSO NO KAMI'S BLOODTHIRST.

YET, DESPITE NIKOTUCHI'S BEST EFFORT, BY THE NEXT MORNING HIS GREAT ARMY HAD FALLEN TO THE DEMON-WARRIOR.

IN THE END, ONLY A HANDFUL WERE LEFT STANDING--

--AND THOSE ABLE MADE A HASTY RETREAT.

FORGIVE US FISHERMAN,--

--IF A WHOLE ARMY CANNOT DEFEAT HOSO NO KAMI, THERE IS INDEED NO HOPE.

TWICE, I HAVE DEFEATED YOUR NIKOTUCHI IN BATTLE. I HAVE PROVEN MYSELF AS A WARRIOR.

YET, YOU CONTINUE TO DENY ME AS YOUR HUSBAND! I GIVE YOU ONE FINAL CHOICE. EITHER ACCEPT MY PROPOSAL OF MARRIAGE--

--OR FACE THIS.

"I STOLE THIS SWORD FROM YOUR HUSBAND IN BATTLE. I HOPE, UNLIKE NIKOTUCHI, YOU WOULD--

"--CHOOSE ME OVER DEATH."

NIKOTUCHI...

THE DEMON LAUGHED AS HE LEFT THE ROOM.

IT IS ONLY NOW, I REALIZE MY MISTAKE. YOU **WERE** MY TRUE LOVE. I REGRET HAVING LEFT YOU. HOSO NO KAMI'S SPITE WILL NOT BE SATISFIED FOR WE SHALL BE REJOINED IN DEATH.

BUT JUST AS O HARU SAN RAISED NIKOTUCHI'S BROKEN SWORD TO PLUNGE INTO HER BREAST,--

O HARU SAN, IT IS I, NIKOTUCHI.

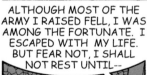

BUT I THOUGHT YOU HAD BEEN SLAIN IN BATTLE.

--A SUDDEN RAPPING CAME FROM THE WALL BEHIND HER.

ALTHOUGH MOST OF THE ARMY I RAISED FELL, I WAS AMONG THE FORTUNATE. I ESCAPED WITH MY LIFE. BUT FEAR NOT, I SHALL NOT REST UNTIL--

--YOU ARE FREE ONCE MORE.

BUT YOU SHALL BE KILLED...

SOON, O HARU SAN began to cry. I CANNOT ALLOW YOU TO SACRIFICE YOURSELF FOR THE SAKE OF MY OWN FREEDOM.

BUT UNLIKE THE TEARS SHE WEPT IN HER HUSBAND'S GARDEN, INSTEAD OF FORMING A RIVER IN WHICH SHE COULD ESCAPE,--

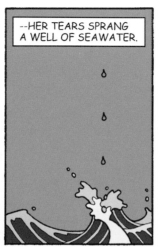

--HER TEARS SPRANG A WELL OF SEAWATER.

EVEN IF YOU FREE ME, I KNOW THAT AS LONG AS I LIVE,--

"--YOU SHALL NEVER BE SAFE FROM THE VENGEFUL GRASP OF HOSO NO KAMI."

AS THE COLD WATER QUICKLY ROSE IN HER PRISON ROOM,--

--SHE PLUGGED THE CHINK IN THE WALL WITH NIKOTUCHI'S SWORD--

--AND ALLOWED HERSELF TO DROWN IN A GREAT SEA OF TEARS.

O HARU SAN?

O HARU SAN?!

33

ALARMED THAT HE COULD NO LONGER HEAR O HARU SAN, NIKOTUCHI BEGAN TO PANIC.

O HARU SAN, WHY WON'T YOU SPEAK TO ME?

HIS FEARS GREW EVEN MORE WHEN HE HEARD THE SOUND OF RUSHING WATER COMING FROM BEHIND THE WALL.

OH NO!

WITH LITTLE HOPE OF EVER REACHING HIS WIFE,--

--NIKOTUCHI DESPERATLEY BEGAN TO CLAW AT THE THICK STONE.

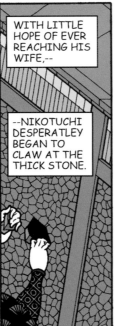

As O HARU SAN'S TEARS SWIFTLY FILLED THE IMMENSE FORTRESS FROM WITHIN, HE CONTINUED TO DIG AT THE GREAT WALL.

BUT EVENTUALLY, HE DID BEGIN TO SEE PROGRESS IN HIS WORK, SLOWLY CHIPPING AWAY AT THE TINY CHINK IN THE FORTRESS--

--UNTIL...

"O HARU SAN!"

O HARU SAN HAD ESCAPED BEING WASHED AWAY BY CLINGING TO THE BROKEN SWORD LODGED IN THE ROCK WALL.

"I THOUGHT I HAD LOST YOU," NIKOTUCHI CRIED.

AND JUST AS HE TOOK HER INTO HIS ARMS, THE FORTRESS WALL GAVE WAY TO THE FLOOD.

FEAR NOT, FOR TOGETHER, WE ARE SAFE--

AN ANGRY RUMBLING CAME FROM BEHIND THEM,--

--AS THE FORTRESS CAME TUMBLING TO THE GROUND,--

--CRUSHING THE DEMON HOSO NO KAMI IN A GREAT PILE OF RUBBLE.

"--AND FROM THIS DAY, I SHALL ALWAYS BE WITH YOU."

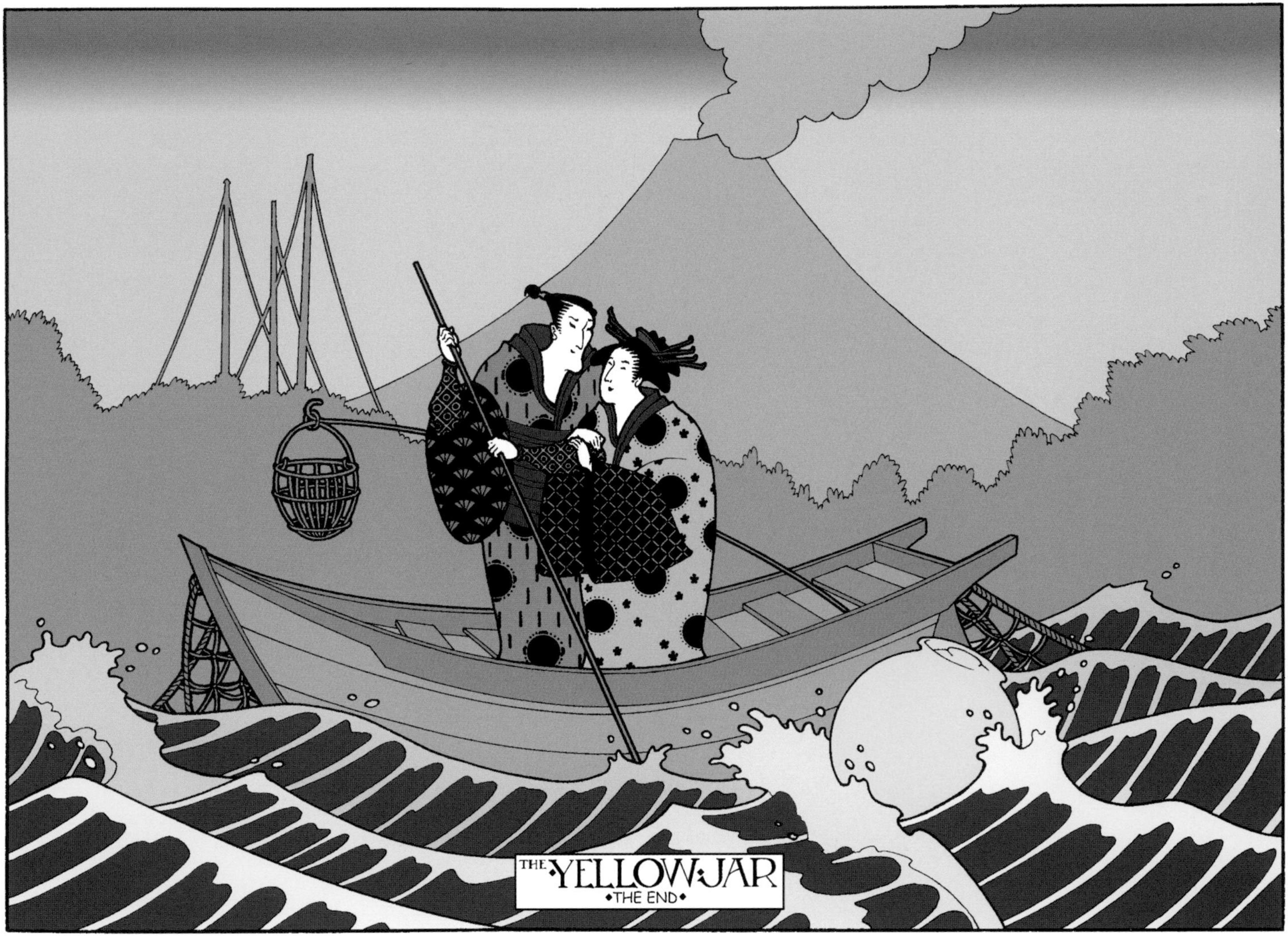
THE YELLOW JAR
THE END

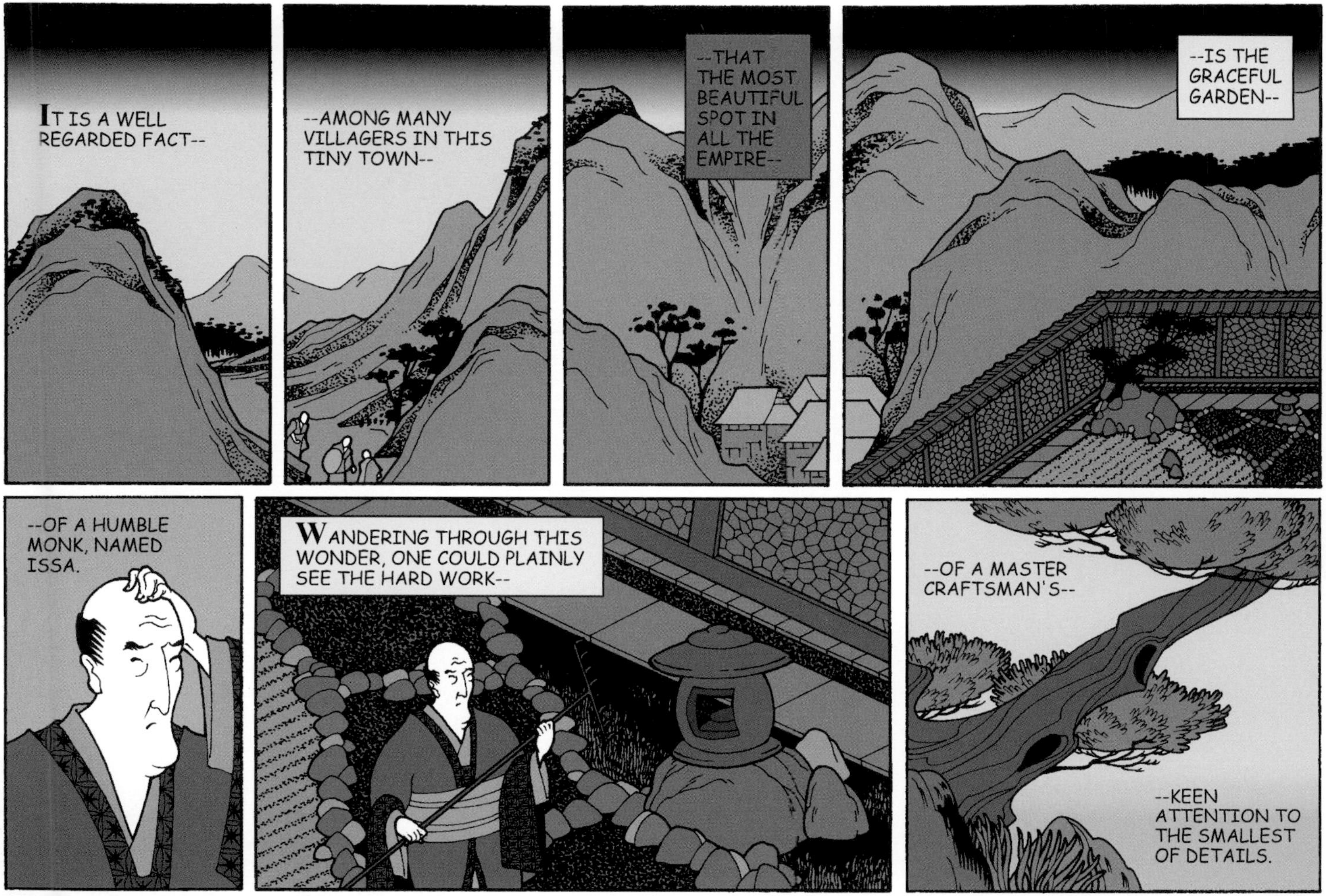
IT IS A WELL REGARDED FACT--
--AMONG MANY VILLAGERS IN THIS TINY TOWN--
--THAT THE MOST BEAUTIFUL SPOT IN ALL THE EMPIRE--
--IS THE GRACEFUL GARDEN--
--OF A HUMBLE MONK, NAMED ISSA.
WANDERING THROUGH THIS WONDER, ONE COULD PLAINLY SEE THE HARD WORK--
--OF A MASTER CRAFTSMAN'S--
--KEEN ATTENTION TO THE SMALLEST OF DETAILS.

TWO·CHRYSANTHEMUM·MAIDENS

So it came as great surprise and distress--

--That one day,--

--Two weeds would appear--

YOU WERE RIGHT, DEAR SISTER...

--Crossing his neatly manicured pebble lawn.

...THIS IS INDEED THE MOST LOVELY GARDEN.

AH YES, IT WILL CERTAINLY MAKE FOR A CHARMING HOME.

Not wanting to disturb his garden, which had just been freshly raked that morning,--

--The monk thought he could convince the weeds to move elsewhere.

...SO AS YOU SEE, THIS BEING SUCH A TINY GARDEN, IT COULDN'T POSSIBLY MAKE FOR A PROPER HOME...

BUT THE TWO WEEDS COULD NOT BE COAXED INTO LEAVING.

OH, DON'T BE SILLY!

THERE IS PLENTY OF ROOM HERE.

INSTEAD, THEY HAPPILY TOOK ROOT IN THE CENTER OF HIS LAWN.

AND THEN, THE MONK THOUGHT,--

PERHAPS, IF I LEAVE THEM ALONE, THEY WILL BORE AND EVENTUALLY LEAVE.

SO, HE WAITED, WEEKS PASSED BY AND STILL THE WEEDS DID NOT LEAVE.

THEY SEEMED QUITE CONTENT TO BE LEFT ALONE IN THEIR NEW HOME.

IF BOREDOM DOES NOT CONVINCE THE WEEDS TO LEAVE, I SHALL ANNOY THEM WITH KINDNESS.

So OVER THE NEXT FEW DAYS, THE MONK--

--TRIED HIS BEST TO BE UNBEARABLY ATTENTIVE.

I HOPE I'M NOT OVER-WATERING YOU.

OH NO, THIS IS REFRESHING.

HMMM... OVERWATERING DOESN'T SEEM TO WORK.

YET DESPITE HOW MUCH HE WOULD WATER,--

--PRUNE--

--OR RAKE AT THEIR ROOTS,--

--HE COULD NOT GET THE TWO STUBBORN WEEDS TO LEAVE HIS GARDEN.

BUT ONE DAY, WHILE TENDING TO HIS LAWN AS HE DID EVERY MORNING, ISSA HAD DISCOVERED,--

--MUCH TO HIS SUPRISE,--

MY WORD!

--THAT THE BOTHER-SOME WEEDS HE ONCE HAD TRIED TO SHUN FROM HIS GARDEN--

--HAD BEGUN TO SPROUT TWO BLOOMS OF MOST UNUSUAL DISTINCTION--

--ONE YELLOW AND ONE WHITE.

THE WEEDS HAD IN FACT BLOSSOMED INTO TWO OF THE MOST BEAUTIFUL CHRYSANTHEMUMS THAT THE OLD MONK HAD EVER SEEN.

AH! WHAT REGAL FORM, THESE FLOWERS OF HUMBLE SOIL. WHAT A FOOL I'VE BEEN!

THE MONK HAD BECOME SO FOND OF THE TWO CHRYSANTHE-MUMS--

--THAT HE EVEN CARVED OUT A SPECIAL SPOT FOR THEM IN HIS LAWN.

THE TWO HAPPILY BECAME THE MAIN ATTRACTION--

--IN THE CENTER OF THE MONK'S PRIZED GARDEN.

TALES OF THE TWO BLOSSOM'S BEAUTY HAD BROUGHT MANY VILLAGERS, SOME OF WHOM TRAVELLED MANY MILES--

--JUST TO SEE ISSA'S FABLED FLOWERS.

OH, THEN THE STORIES ARE TRUE!

THEY ARE INDEED THE MOST LOVELY BLOOMS I'VE EVER SEEN. I THINK I AM GOING TO CRY!

THE VILLAGERS EXCLAIMED IN ADORATION.

THE TWO WERE STARS.

BUT DESPITE THE VILLAGER'S ADMIRATION AND CONSTANT COMPLIMENTS FOR BOTH THE CHRYSANTHEMUMS,--

--IT SOON BECAME QUITE CLEAR THAT--

--THEY PREFERED ONE FLOWER OVER THE OTHER.

BOTH ARE LOVELY BUT ONE IS FAR MORE BEAUTIFUL.

IT'S EVEN MORE BEAUTIFUL NEXT TO THE FLAWED WHITE BLOSSOM.

THE YELLOW FLOWER RESEMBLES THE PERFECT FACE OF A SUN.

TO WITNESS ITS VIBRANCE IS TRULY A JOYOUS EXPERIENCE.

SO THE MONK SEPARATED THE TWO CHRYSANTHEMUMS.

GOODBYE, DEAR SISTER.

BUT WHAT ABOUT ME?

43

FOR BEING FAR MORE FAIR THAN HER SISTER,--

--THE YELLOW BLOSSOM WAS GIVEN A SPECIAL SPOT IN THE MONK'S GARDEN,--

--SO THAT SHE MAY EASILY BE ADMIRED BY THE VILLAGERS.

PROTECTED FROM THE SUN AND WITH HER ROOTS ADORNED BY BRIGHTLY COLORED LEAVES, THE YELLOW CHRYSANTHEMUM'S ALMOST EVERY NEED WAS ATTENDED.

EVERY NEED BUT FOR ONE SECRET WISH, FOR NO MATTER HOW OFTEN THE TOWNSFOLK CAME TO CODDLE HER,--

SIGH.

--SHE STILL WAS VERY SAD.

FOR HOW COULD SHE BE TRULY HAPPY WITHOUT THE COMPANY OF HER SISTER?

THE FOLLOWING WINTER WAS ESPECIALLY HARD ON THE WHITE BLOSSOM.

UNLIKE HER SISTER, WHO WAS GIVEN AUTUMN LEAVES TO KEEP WARM,--

--SHE HAD NOTHING.

THE HARSH FROST HAD TURNED HER PALER AND PALER.

THE COLD KEPT THE VILLAGERS FROM VISITING--

--AND ISSA HAD LONG FORGOTTEN TO TEND TO HER.

SOON, THE WHITE CHRYSANTHEMUM GREW SICK AND LONELY.

THE BITTER WINTER HAD FROZEN OVER THE MONK'S GARDEN.

IN HER ILL HEALTH, THE WHITE BLOSSOM TRIED TO STAND THE SEASONAL STORMS.

WINTER'S CALLOUS FROST WITHERS THIS ONCE PROUD FLOWER. TO IT, I SUCCUMB.

EVENTUALLY, THE STORMS DID PASS AND IT WAS LATE IN THE SEASON WHEN THE GARDEN RECEIVED A MYSTERIOUS VISITOR.

HE INTRODUCED HIMSELF AS THE SECOND SON OF A GREAT AND NOBLE FAMILY.

I HAVE BEEN SENT BY MY FATHER IN SEARCH OF A SYMBOL FOR OUR NEW FAMILY CREST.

AH, THEN YOU'VE COME TO THE RIGHT PLACE, DEAR TRAVELER.

IT HAS BEEN RUMORED THAT YOUR GARDEN, ABOVE ALL OTHERS IN THE EMPIRE, IS THE MOST BEAUTIFUL.

"I HAVE COME A GREAT DISTANCE TO SEE FOR MYSELF ITS BEAUTY."

"HERE, I HOPE TO FIND A SYMBOL THAT WOULD BEST REPRESENT THE NOBILITY OF MY FAMILY."

HAPPILY, THE MONK SHOWED THE YOUNG NOBLEMAN HIS GARDEN.

I'VE THE LOVELIEST FLOWER TO SHOW YOU.

BUT TO ISSA'S SUPRISE, HIS GUEST OVERLOOKED THE PRIZED YELLOW CHRYSANTHEMUM--

WHAT IS THIS?

--WHEN HE SAW SOMETHING HIDDEN IN THE SNOWY LAWN.

THIS TINY BLOSSOM, SO WHITE IT WAS ALMOST UNSEEN IN THE SNOW.

"LIKE MYSELF, IT HAD BRAVED THE BITTER WINTER ALONE."

"WHAT SOMBER BEAUTY, SHE WILL BE A FITTING SYMBOL."

"A DISCARDED FLOWER FOR A SECOND SON."

"HAD I NOT BEEN SO BLIND AND NEGLECTED MY DUTIES AS A GARDENER THIS NEVER WOULD HAVE HAPPENED."

PLEADING FOR FORGIVENESS, THE OLD MONK BEGGED,--

"PLEASE, TAKE THE BLOSSOM FOR YOUR OWN."

SO THE NOBLEMAN NURSED THE LITTLE WHITE FLOWER BACK TO HEALTH--

--AND ADOPTED HER IMAGE AS HIS CREST.

AND LIKE HER FAVORED SISTER, THE YELLOW BLOSSOM,--

--SO TOO WAS THE POOR WHITE CHRYSANTHEMUM GIVEN HER RIGHTFUL PLACE OF HONOR.

THE END